SUMMARY & ANALYSIS

OF

FANATICAL PROSPECTING

THE ULTIMATE GUIDE TO OPENING SALES
CONVERSATIONS AND FILLING THE PIPELINE
BY LEVERAGING SOCIAL SELLING, TELEPHONE,
E-MAIL, TEXT, AND COLD CALLING

A GUIDE TO THE BOOK
BY JEB BLOUNT

BY **ZIP**READS

NOTE: This book is a summary and analysis and is meant as a companion to, not a replacement for, the original book.
Please follow this link to purchase a copy of the original book from Amazon: https://amzn.to/2IA5nRG

Copyright © 2018 by ZIP Reads. All rights reserved. This book or parts thereof may not be reproduced in any form, stored in any retrieval system, or transmitted in any form by any means—electronic, mechanical, photocopy, recording, or otherwise—without prior written permission of the publisher, except as provided by United States of America copyright law. This book is intended as a companion to, not a replacement for the original book. ZIP Reads is wholly responsible for this content and is not associated with the original author in any way.

TABLE OF CONTENTS

SYNOPSIS 6
CHAPTER SUMMARIES 8

Chapter 1: Why Prospecting Matters 8

Chapter 2: How a Fanatical Prospector Thinks 8

Chapter 3: The Case for Cold Calling 9

Chapter 4: Successful Prospecting Requires Balance 10

Chapter 5: The Three Laws of Prospecting 10

Chapter 6: Don't Underestimate the Power of Data 11

Chapter 7: The Three Ps 11

Chapter 8: Time Management Differentiates 12

Chapter 9: Know What Your Objective Is 13

Chapter 10: the Prospecting Pyramid 13

Chapter 11: Why You Should Be Using a CRM 14

Chapter 12: Familiarity is Key 15

Chapter 13: Social Media as a Sales Tool 15

Chapter 14: The Power of Tailored Messaging 16

Chapter 15: How to Be Great on the Phone 17

Chapter 16: Dealing with Rejection 18

Chapter 17: Getting Past the Secretary 19

Chapter 18: In-Person Prospecting 19

Chapter 19: E-Mail Prospecting 20

Chapter 20: Text Messaging 20

Chapter 21: How to Develop Mental Fortitude 21

Chapter 22: One More Call 22

Chapter 23: How Bad Do You Want It? 22

KEY TAKEAWAYS 23

Steps in Building a Sustainable Sales Pipeline 23

Signs That You Are Seeking an Easy Way Out in Sales 23

Designing a Balanced Prospecting Regimen 24

Steps in Overcoming Sales Slumps 24

The Two Critical Ratios in Tracking Sales Performance 25

How Top Performers Emulate CEOs................................... 25

How to Handle Threats to the Golden Hours 26

How to Describe a Database Using a Bell-Shaped Curve ... 26

How to Set Prospecting Objectives Using the Bell Curve 27

How to Filter Your Database and Create Powerful Prospecting Lists.. 27

What a CRM Does for the Salesperson 28

Types of Referrals and How to Generate Referrals 28

The Double Edge of Social Selling 29

Objectives of Social Prospecting 29

What Prospects Will Give Up Their Time For 30

Five Step Tele-Prospecting Framework 30

The Three-Step Framework for Handling Rejection 31

Tips on How to Get the Details of a Prospect in the Face of an Impenetrable Gatekeeper 32

Why Salespeople Make IPP a Primary Prospecting Approach 32

Planning for E-Mail Prospecting 33

How to Structure Effective Text Messages 34

Four Pillars of Mental Toughness in Sales........................... 34

EDITORIAL REVIEW 36
BACKGROUND ON AUTHOR 38

SYNOPSIS

In the book *Fanatical Prospecting*, Jeb Blount is both a coach and a motivator. He begins by addressing the salesperson by dissecting the elements of extraordinary salespeople and what sets them apart. Blount discloses what it takes to move from a mediocre salesperson to a top performer. Also, he sets the stage with an affirmation of the importance of prospecting and why relentless prospecting is crucial in sales.

Assertively, he challenges the simmering argument that prospecting, more precisely telephone prospecting, is dead, dying or "old school" and other excuses for not prospecting. He emphasizes that salespeople must apply a cocktail of prospecting approaches and adhere to the fundamental laws of prospecting. Diverging from the typical belief that sales is an art only, the book underscores the importance of keeping tabs with the numbers. Also, he expertly tackles several personal issues that hinder salespeople from attaining superstar status.

From the salesperson to actual prospecting, Blount describes the prospecting pyramid and how it is indispensable for salespeople. Also, he delves into the benefits of a CRM and why it is imperative for salespeople to change their attitudes about CRMs. Salespeople and sales leaders will also enjoy the in-depth explanations on how to leverage social media and how the concept of familiarity works. Moreover, the book provides insight on how to coin the right messages during prospecting endeavors.

Throughout the book, Blount reiterates the importance of persistence in prospecting. He focuses on four approaches to prospecting and digs deep into telephone prospecting describing it as the most efficient and productive tool in sales. He elaborates the challenges that salespeople experience during telephone prospecting and specifically expounds more on how to handle gatekeepers. Blount also provides excellent insight into the other three types of prospecting and reiterates that no single approach is sufficient by itself. Instead, a salesperson should adopt a balanced approach.

To conclude, Blount systematically identifies and describes personal traits that are consistent with all top performers. He observes that the traits are not innate qualities—anyone can acquire them. He closes by revealing his mantra, the words that transformed him to become a top performer and the question that drives and replays in the minds of every superstar salesperson.

All in all, *Fanatical Prospecting* is an exciting, insightful read that will teach you how to make your selling endeavors more efficient, more productive, and super rewarding.

CHAPTER SUMMARIES

CHAPTER 1: WHY PROSPECTING MATTERS

There are mediocre salespeople, ordinary sales people and superstars. Superstars are the 20 percent cream of sales teams who rake in 80 percent of the sales and sweep up all the commissions and awards. They are not one hit wonders and don't have superior skills or exceptional talent, but their secret is being relentless in prospecting.

Superstars are fanatical about prospecting and they don't make excuses, complain, whine, live in fear, or procrastinate. They prospect in good seasons and during awful seasons. They prospect even when they don't feel like doing it, knowing that it's the golden goose that keeps their pipelines full. Their daily mantra is "one more call."

Although prospecting is not painless and sometimes it's truly difficult, as you read, you'll learn how to increase your efficacy, productivity, and ultimately know how to get over the drag and keep going.

CHAPTER 2: HOW A FANATICAL PROSPECTOR THINKS

What is different about the superstars? An excellent way of describing the differentiator is using Dr. Carol S. Dweck's concept of mindset. Fanatical prospectors adopt a mindset that thrives and does not wane in the face of adversity. They are optimistic and enthusiastic, shielding themselves against the nay-sayers, and on a low day, they reach deep into their reservoirs for stored-up enthusiasm. Also, they are competitive and fervent. They are confident and self-controlled expecting nothing but conversion. They know how to manage their emotions. Fanatical prospectors are persistent and have an unquenchable thirst for knowledge. They don't operate in chaos but are systematic and efficient, making the most of their available time and jealously guarding their "golden hours." They are flexible, open to adopting new techniques, quick to adapt working strategies and keen to become adept with new techniques. They do whatever it takes to keep their pipelines full.

CHAPTER 3: THE CASE FOR COLD CALLING

People who suggest that cold calling is an old-school strategy that doesn't work often want to cross-sell a "secret working formula" that promises to take away the hard work and fill your sales pipeline with little effort. There has been a proliferation of self-proclaimed cold calling experts who promise wonder formulas to eliminate rejection. However, they all miss the point. It's not about cold calling, or whatever the degree is (warm, hot, lukewarm), but about your willingness to interrupt a prospect when they least expect it. Interruption almost always results in an automatic rejection as a first reaction, and everyone abhors rejections. However, your willingness to interrupt is the key to successful prospecting, and without a constant desire to disrupt your prospect, your sales pipelines will dry up. Therefore, the question is not to cold call or not to cold call. Instead, ask how you can skillfully balance your prospecting approaches and edge out your competitors.

CHAPTER 4: SUCCESSFUL PROSPECTING REQUIRES BALANCE

Another threat to the sales pipeline is buying into the fallacy that a single method for prospecting is sufficient. It's a death wish in a sales career—just like you wouldn't pour your entire retirement into a single stock. Diversification of your prospecting strategies and designing your balance to suit your unique situation gives you an advantage. Having a balanced approach is a fundamental sales principle applicable in all industries, products, services or geographies.

CHAPTER 5: THE THREE LAWS OF PROSPECTING

It is imperative for salespeople to adhere to the three fundamental laws of prospecting so as to be certain an ever-full pipeline. They are the Universal Law of Need, the Thirty-Day Rule and the Law of Replacement. The universal law of need asserts that the more you need something, the less likely you are to get it. Dire need drives desperation, which eventually magnifies and accelerates failure. When you are inconsistent and procrastinate with prospecting, you set yourself up for dire need and subsequent distress. However, developing the discipline of prospecting daily nurtures the opposite. The thirty-day rule postulates that today's prospecting will pay off in the next ninety days. When you ignore prospecting for any reason, it will come back to haunt you in the form of a dry pipeline. Thirdly, the law of replacement demands that you must replace prospects based on your closing ratio and continually push for new opportunities.

CHAPTER 6: DON'T UNDERESTIMATE THE POWER OF DATA

Selling has a scientific aspect to it. There are certain principles and formulas, which when followed, guarantee successful outcomes. Yes, selling is mathematical. However, there's a common belief that sales do not involve numbers, which is a far cry from the truth. The bottom line is that sales are hardwired in the numbers, and there is a simple formula that states what (quality) you put into the pipeline and how much (quantity) determine the output. Superstar salespeople know that this formula works, and they keep their fingers on the pulse of their numbers. It keeps them grounded in reality and focused on their daily goals. It ensures a salesperson is honest in their self-appraisal and not delusional about their performance.

CHAPTER 7: THE THREE Ps

Procrastination, perfectionism and paralysis of analysis are the three Ps that hold salespeople from efficient and effective prospecting. Procrastination is the failure to take daily action while deluding yourself that you'll get to it later. Perfectionism happens when you want to get all your prospects perfectly lined up before you begin calling. You deceive yourself that you are working, and it generates both procrastination and fear of failure. Perfectionism is a killer for any prospecting. Paralysis from analysis happens when salespeople entangle prospecting opportunities with many "what if" questions rather than just going ahead to undertake the prospecting activity and let the "what ifs" handle themselves. All salespeople are susceptible to these three Ps. However, with a good coach anyone can overcome them.

CHAPTER 8: TIME MANAGEMENT DIFFERENTIATES

In addition to the three Ps, salespeople also grapple with time management. Whereas superstar salespeople are masters at maximizing their prime selling time, average and mediocre salespeople struggle with time management. Top performers plan their days such that each activity has a separate time block. During the time block, they focus entirely on a specific action giving no room for distractions.

The "golden hours" are the prime selling hours for a salesperson. How well they can manage these hours defines their eventual success or failure. Time blocking works wonders especially when it comes to prospecting. For instance, an hour each day focused on sheer telephone prospecting, an hour for email prospecting, and another hour for social prospecting is guaranteed to jam pack any pipeline in less than two months. Block off your prospecting hours and do not compromise that time with any other activities. When you calculate your worth during your prime selling time, it illuminates how trivial these other non-selling activities are and can guide you in making choices on how to make the most out of your time.

CHAPTER 9: KNOW WHAT YOUR OBJECTIVE IS

Blocking off your golden hours is essential, but knowing your objective is critical during prospecting. It makes a salesperson more efficient and effective. There are four core objectives of prospecting: setting an appointment, gathering information and qualifying, closing a sale, and building familiarity.

The degree of importance of these prospecting objectives vary with industry, prospect base, product and service. Objective setting helps salespeople to avoid stumbling on a series of unqualified prospects. It helps them become laser focused on what they want and ask for it rather than engage in small talk, chit-chat and long-winded scripts. Top performers filter through their databases, set their objectives, spend little or no time with non-buyers, and move swiftly to close qualified prospects. It requires poise, confidence and mastery of the sales process.

CHAPTER 10: THE PROSPECTING PYRAMID

Organizing your database according to your objectives is the first step in refining it. An excellent tool to further refine your prospecting objectives is the prospecting pyramid. Not every prospect is the same, and as such, salespeople have to be systematic, treat them differently and keep refining their goals when attacking the database.

Star performers optimize their efficiency and effectiveness by organizing their prospecting block and aligning the golden hours with highly qualified prospects who are in the buying window. In order to achieve this, top performers organize their prospect databases as a pyramid with the highest priority coming on top. They proceed to the other prospects after expending their best energy with the candidates most likely to buy. Building an effective and robust prospecting pyramid takes consistent and disciplined effort. However, a healthy list yields potent results.

CHAPTER 11: WHY YOU SHOULD BE USING A CRM

Many salespeople abhor CRMs. However, the undeniable truth is that a CRM can help you build powerful prospecting lists. An organized prospect database is the most potent weapon any salesperson can have in their arsenal. Average and mediocre salespeople see CRMs as a bother. They see tasks such as updating details as duties meant for the company, and not for their benefit. However, winners know the importance of the CRMs, and they take up related tasks like the CEO of their territory. They build information on databases like a jigsaw puzzle, putting in considerable effort to gather and build information and recognizing the small wins. They put every detail into account, make clear notes, never procrastinate, and develop the discipline to do it right the first time. They do all this because they know that it will pay off over time.

CHAPTER 12: FAMILIARITY IS KEY

The CRM also helps salespeople to learn more about their prospects as they nurture them to higher levels of the pyramid. But, what makes a total stranger move from being an uninterested party to a viable prospect? Familiarity with the salesperson.

When prospecting, familiarity doesn't breed contempt, on the contrary, it builds trust. Familiarity lubricates the prospecting efforts and builds future business. As prospects become more familiar with the salesperson and the brand, they develop trust. The trust can grow to levels where prospects communicate freely without considering it an intrusion. At this point, the salesperson will have attained the familiarity threshold.

Attaining the familiarity threshold takes significant investment in time, intellect, emotion, energy and technology. However, it pays off big time. Salespeople can build and accelerate familiarity by leveraging on persistent and consistent prospecting, through referrals and introductions, through networking, and by riding on a company brand or their personal brand. However, superstars are careful not to spend too much time building familiarity while foregoing the crucial task of meeting the day's sales. They balance the need for sales today with efforts to invest in the future.

CHAPTER 13: SOCIAL MEDIA AS A SALES TOOL

A modern and powerful way of building familiarity is through social media. Social selling is a prominent, must-have, tool in sales. *Social media is the most significant technological advancement since the telephone* (Blount, p. 105). It allows salespeople to tap into, analyze, and utilize an unprecedented amount of data in no time. Top performers know how indispensable social media is and they adopt social selling tactics as part of their arsenal. They are willing to pay the price to learn how to access and become more effective and efficient on social platforms. They begin by appreciating the core objectives of social prospecting and comprehend the characteristics of effective social prospecting. They get a firm understanding of the different categories of social selling tools and employ them appropriately.

Social selling is best when woven into a balanced prospecting effort rather than an exclusive channel. People prefer to connect, interact and learn on social media. Thus social prospecting is an excellent avenue for building familiarity, lead nurturing, doing research, and for subtle inbound prospecting.

CHAPTER 14: THE POWER OF TAILORED MESSAGING

Social selling and familiarity will bring a salesperson to the waters abounding with prospects. However, reeling in the prospects requires skill. Every salesperson craves magical words that can wow a prospect into total submission but that's just a fallacy, and such words don't exist. Nevertheless, it is possible to craft messages that can impact and move prospects towards action. Prospecting messages need not be complicated but should have one clear objective: to persuade a prospect to give you their time. To achieve this, salespeople must plug into the prospect's psychology, develop the right mindset, and have mental sturdiness. Prospects often want messages that are quick, clear and simple, and relevant to their situation. In other words, salespeople should look to answer the question, pondering in every prospect's mind, "what's in it for me?" Therefore the message must solve the prospect's issues, use the prospect's language, and offer competitive differentiators. However, you should also be conscious that the focus of prospecting is to get the prospect to give a foothold of their time. After securing the appointment, the solutions can come later.

When bridging a solution, the salesperson should consider that people are first emotional before they are logical. Then follow to qualify the prospect and ask what they want. Once they have asked they should pause for a response confidently knowing that the rule of thirds is in their favor.

CHAPTER 15: HOW TO BE GREAT ON THE PHONE

What is the best way of communicating a compelling message and triggering action from a prospect? A face-to-face encounter would do. However, it's not the most efficient. A phone call is more efficient and just as effective. However, most salespeople abhor the thought of picking up the phone to interrupt a prospect. They find it awkward because they have no clue what to say and ramble on or regurgitate annoying scripts that elicit resistance and rejection. Moreover, mediocre salespeople can hardly deal with rebuttals and are afraid of rejection. Despite all these challenges, many companies overlook the need to train their salespeople on telephone prospecting and hire sales team leaders who have no clue on how to coach team members to master these skills. However, determined salespeople can learn how to structure a call and what to do and say when on the line with a prospect. Structured calls help superstars to leverage the telephone and maximize their golden hours. Telephone prospecting is best when scheduled during a phone block and prioritized in the early hours of a sales day.

CHAPTER 16: DEALING WITH REJECTION

Prospecting is not a favorite activity of most because it is a place of vulnerability. People abhor prospecting because they fear rejection. Rejection is a strong de-motivator. Salespeople feel it every time a prospect has a reflex response, brush-off or an objection. However, it is possible to learn how to deal with rejection. Dealing with rejection is not about intellectualizing, downplaying or denying it. Instead, it's about learning to manage and disrupt the negative emotions it triggers. By mastering how to deal with rejection, you can turn the tables around, interrupt the prospect's thought path, and win them over. However, there are occasions when a prospect blatantly hurls insults. Rather than spiral into self-destruction or persist on beating a dead horse, find a way that will use that anger energy positively.

CHAPTER 17: GETTING PAST THE SECRETARY

One of the most common sources of rejection when prospecting is gatekeepers such as receptionists and assistants. They hold the precarious role of protecting the prospect's time. Therefore, one of their jobs is to say no to salespeople. However, you can succeed in handling gatekeepers. First, keep in mind that gatekeepers are just as human as you are and they have emotions. Therefore, a cocktail of good manners, likeability, and people-savviness will give you an edge.

Whereas there's no secret formula to get through or around gatekeepers, here are some tips that will help you in dealing with them. First be likeable and cordial, use the word please, be transparent, connect with the gatekeeper, avoid tricks or schemes; be creative and throw in some humor. If these tips don't work, you can change the game and sidestep the gatekeeper.

CHAPTER 18: IN-PERSON PROSPECTING

In-person prospecting is an essential part of a balanced prospecting strategy, and it works best with residential and business to business sales. However, it is also the least efficient approach and should be used only to supplement or complement other methods such as telephone and social prospecting. The primary objective of in person prospecting is to gather qualifying information and enrich the database. Before you set out for an in person prospecting expedition, ensure that you research thoroughly, master the sales process, and are prepared to close. When out there, don't be myopic or blind to other opportunities. Instead, be acutely aware of every opportunity that surrounds you.

CHAPTER 19: E-MAIL PROSPECTING

E-mail prospecting is also a powerful addition to a balanced prospecting strategy. When done right, it can generate more engagement and responses than social prospecting. However, when done wrong or without thought, you risk a prospect blocking you permanently. For e-mail prospecting to work, it must follow the three fundamental rules. First, your email must get delivered. Second, your email must get opened and third, your email must convert. Therefore, salespeople must take time to research and plan. You must consider the audience and reflect on what makes an effective email. Most importantly, keep practicing. Coining the right words is not easy, but with enough practice, the right messages will be rolling off your fingertips. Armed with the right message, you can then send the email at the most opportune time. However, before you click the send button, check for typos and grammar issues which could water down your efforts in an instant.

CHAPTER 20: TEXT MESSAGING

Many people detest the thought of receiving unsolicited sales pitches through text messaging. Text messages have over the years evolved to be a haven, where people can communicate with family and friends without the bombardment of spam and ads. However, this is the very reason why text messages are such a potent prospecting tool. Before you consider text messages, it is important to note that familiarity is critical. Otherwise, texting a prospect could do more harm than good. Text messages work because they have a high response rate, which in sales translates to a higher probability of conversion. You can use texts to anchor conversations after networking events, reach out to a prospect after a trigger event, build up prospects for future business, and create opportunities for engagements. Ultimately, text prospecting is best used to strengthen relationships with already familiar prospects.

CHAPTER 21: HOW TO DEVELOP MENTAL FORTITUDE

Having looked at the prime prospecting tools, they would amount to nothing without mental toughness. *Mental toughness is the ability to get back up when you've been knocked down and be resilient in the face of rejection* (Blount, p 249). Top performers keep winning because of mental toughness. It is founded on self-confidence, attention control, ability to minimize negative energy, maintain motivation levels, attitude control, and visual and imagery control. Mental toughness is not inborn; it can be acquired by changing your mindset and progressively altering your strategies. Add faith to keep you focused on your goals and persistence. Top performers exemplify mental toughness and add to it optimism, competitiveness and an insatiable drive for achievement. They feed their attitudes with positive beliefs and an expectation to win. They are always aware of their attitudes, tuning them to the right channel. When they win, they bask in the glory of achievement for only a moment before returning to their next sale and seeking ways to improve.

CHAPTER 22: ONE MORE CALL

There is a sales mantra that works for superstar salespeople because they have the discipline to do it and don't waver: "one more call." The extra calls have a profound impact when followed through without fail. They give top performers the edge. Like all other salespeople, superstar salespeople experience all the emotions that pull them towards giving up. However, they understand that they pay for success with hard work and making that one extra call.

CHAPTER 23: HOW BAD DO YOU WANT IT?

In sales, there will always be an overwhelming challenge to overcome, a mountain to climb or target to meet. You may have prepared for eternity and concocted many strategies. However, when push comes to shove, the only question that matters is, how bad do you want it? It determines what you'll do to achieve excellence.

KEY TAKEAWAYS

STEPS IN BUILDING A SUSTAINABLE SALES PIPELINE

Many theories have recently come up underestimating the importance of prospecting. However, poor prospecting, or a lack thereof is the most significant reason why sales teams fail. Businesses grapple with dry pipelines not because there is a deficiency in talent or due to poor strategy but because their sales teams stopped prospecting.

For any sales team or salesperson to move from mediocrity and build an endless sales pipeline they must first acknowledge the truth that prospecting is hard and discard the emotional need to find an easy way out. Secondly, they must keep it real and focus on the three things that they have control over, their actions, reactions and their mindset.

SIGNS THAT YOU ARE SEEKING AN EASY WAY OUT IN SALES

It is difficult and awkward to interrupt someone's day. It makes a salesperson vulnerable and triggers the fear of rejection. However, not giving in to the fear and persisting in your quest for one more call is what separates superstar salespeople from mediocre salespeople. The following are tell-tell signs that mark the downward slide into mediocrity.

- Finding all manner of excuses not to prospect
- When you incessantly dwell on the unknown

- Over-analyzing prospects with the intent to line them in perfect order rather than just reaching out

DESIGNING A BALANCED PROSPECTING REGIMEN

When developing a prospecting schedule, be careful that you don't overly rely on a single prospecting approach. A balanced regimen consists of a cocktail of various prospecting channels, and distribution of prospecting time, resources and methodology with what works best for your industry, product, the complexity of the deal, your customer base and your tenure in the territory.

STEPS IN OVERCOMING SALES SLUMPS

Salespeople often experience slumps. It happens when they have either ignored or overlooked one or more of the fundamental laws of prospecting. However, a recession doesn't have to be the death knell of a sales job or a sales career. When experiencing a sales slump, first, observe the rule of holes. "When you find yourself in a hole, stop digging" (Blount, p 33). Quit moping and looking for excuses why you are not selling. Instead, do all it takes to focus your mind and actions on attaining daily targets.

Second, don't fret over what might happen if things don't work out. Worrying cannot change the future but it distorts the present.

Third, put all your energy, emotion, and effort into the three things that you can control: your reaction, your mindset and your actions

Usually, it takes 30 days of dedicated activity to get back on track.

THE TWO CRITICAL RATIOS IN TRACKING SALES PERFORMANCE

Tracking numbers in sales is essential. Consistent tracking enables salespeople to perform honest appraisals. There are two critical ratios in sales: efficiency and effectiveness. These ratios help salespeople to make regular and relevant adjustments based on their performance stats.

Efficiency is how much activity you are generating in the time set aside for prospecting.

Effectiveness, on the other hand, is the ratio between the activity and the outcome.

An efficient and effective sales person is a top performer.

HOW TOP PERFORMERS EMULATE CEOs

Top performing salespeople adopt the mindset of a CEO. They accept that they are entirely responsible for their success or failure and take full ownership of their time, territory, resources and prospects.

Top performers, like CEOs, do not make excuses or blame others for their failures. When faced with hurdles, distractions or unexpected situations, they adapt and find creative solutions to keep the ball rolling towards the objective, filling the sales pipeline.

HOW TO HANDLE THREATS TO THE GOLDEN HOURS

Salespeople, unlike other staff, are paid to get one thing done—to sell. However, this does not immunize them from different roles in the office which demand their time. Some of these roles relate to selling; others don't. However, these activities are not their core functions. When faced with these demanding tasks, salespeople can choose to give in and give up their golden hours, deceiving themselves that they are getting work done, when in reality they are gradually drying up their own pipeline. However, they can also say *no*, which is not easy but is essential in creating boundaries. A more practical approach is learning to prioritize the core function, and doing the non-sales activities before or after the golden hours, during the platinum hours. Another effective way of handling non-sales tasks is by delegating to competent people and checking that the task is done.

HOW TO DESCRIBE A DATABASE USING A BELL-SHAPED CURVE

A bell-shaped curve can explain the distribution of qualified prospects in a database.

There's a small portion of prospects who are fully qualified and ready to buy. A large percentage lie in the qualified zone but won't be buying due to several restrictions. There will also be a significant percentage who are eligible but with inconsistent or incomplete data and there will be a small fraction who will never buy.

HOW TO SET PROSPECTING OBJECTIVES USING THE BELL CURVE

The bell curve gives a salesperson a description of what to generally expect from a database of prospects. With the first fraction of highly qualified prospects, the objective should be to arrange for an appointment. For the second portion of qualified candidates, the goal is nurturing them into the buying window. For the third group who are eligible but have data gaps, your objective should be to gather information as you qualify them. Finally, the salesperson should aim to eliminate the fourth group of "never-buyers" from the database.

HOW TO FILTER YOUR DATABASE AND CREATE POWERFUL PROSPECTING LISTS

Each situation calls for a unique approach to develop a potent prospecting list. You can use different combinations to structure a prospecting list for maximum return.

You can choose to organize the prospects according to prospecting objective, prospecting channel, the qualification level, the potential, the probability of buying, and the territory plan, among others. Getting started with quick wins gives you the impetus to attack the rest of the day, and once you've exhausted your high-potential list, your prospecting activities can move on to nurturing and qualifying the prospects on lower levels of the pyramid.

WHAT A CRM DOES FOR THE SALESPERSON

Building your database in a CRM may seem tedious at first, but it pays off over time. Through persistent prospecting and research, you get a clearer picture of your database which helps you to build on opportunities. CRMs are the most potent weapons in your arsenal because a CRM helps you manage details and tasks from various prospects without having to memorize anything. A CRM keeps salespeople organized. It enables the sorting of prospects and systematic qualification and migration to higher tiers of the prospecting pyramid. Finally, a CRM reminds you of important things to do, and when they are due, keeping you in control.

TYPES OF REFERRALS AND HOW TO GENERATE REFERRALS

A referral or introduction gives you instant credibility to new acquaintances. It's the most powerful and straightforward route to familiarity. Referrals can be from previous customers who had an excellent experience. You can also get personal referrals from your friends and family. Professional referrals come from your peers from diverse professional relationships and networks. References are fertile lairs for future business, and top performers know it. Therefore, they ask for referrals and ensure that they deliver a stellar experience which in turn generates more referrals.

THE DOUBLE EDGE OF SOCIAL SELLING

Technology today enables previously unfathomable connections and interactions to occur. As a salesperson, you have access to and can analyze unlimited amounts of data at incredible speeds. Social media creates a sort of paradox in prospecting. On the one hand, it is a viable way to spruce up a pipeline and accelerate your sales. On the other hand, as the data becomes more available and valuable information becomes costly, the benefits of social selling are blurred by the skyrocketing costs of accessing the data.

OBJECTIVES OF SOCIAL PROSPECTING

Social prospecting is a potent tool for selling. However, like any other tool, salespeople must have a clear-cut aim so that they are effective and get a good return on investment. The first objective of social prospecting is building and improving your brand to enhance efforts in nurturing familiarity and trust. The second objective is to strengthen inbound prospecting capacities through insight and education. The third is to leverage on the information available to power up your strategic prospecting efforts. The fourth aim is to enable more research and information gathering. Finally, the fifth goal is to develop opportunities to engage in outbound prospecting.

WHAT PROSPECTS WILL GIVE UP THEIR TIME FOR

Prospects jealously guard their time. Before they give in to a salesperson's pitch they will dissect the message and assess if it offers them the following:

Emotional Value: Can the salesperson connect with them emotionally through emotions such as stress and anxiety, or offer hope and peace of mind?

Insight value: would the offering give them a competitive advantage either as an individual or an organization?

Tangible (logic) Value: What is the impact of the offering? How much? How many? What results can the solution deliver, or has it provided before?

The best way to coin a message to pitch to a prospect is by first taking their position and looking at issues from their perspective and considering what is most important to them.

FIVE STEP TELE-PROSPECTING FRAMEWORK

Tele-prospecting is a dreaded activity because it has a high rejection rate and all humans naturally detest rejection. However, salespeople can increase their success rate by structuring it with the prospect in mind. The following five-step framework will help you pass across a succinct message that triggers action.

First get the prospect's attention; the best way to do it is my calling them by name.

Second, identify yourself and the reason you called. It demonstrates that you're professional and you value the prospect's time.

Third, bridge their need to your pitch. Link what you want to what is relevant to the prospect.

Fourth, ask for what you want and allow them to respond.

Lastly, be confident, direct and eloquent; don't pause or stutter so that you may maintain control of the conversation.

THE THREE-STEP FRAMEWORK FOR HANDLING REJECTION

Prospecting is not the most enjoyable part of selling. It has a high rate of rejection but, it also bears the highest rewards. Superstar salespeople learn how to handle rejection.

Below is a three-step framework for handling rejection that will help you overcome the pain of rejection, take charge of a conversation, and turn around prospects.

First, use anchoring statements to regain self-composure and logic so that you can handle the emotions that a rejection triggers.

Second, disrupt the prospect's thought pattern. Just as you have an expected "natural" reaction to rejection, the candidate also has predictable expectations. You can ask questions or give responses that disrupt their thought pattern, disarm attempts to resist, and draw them closer to your agenda.

Finally, be assumptive and confident in asking for what you want.

TIPS ON HOW TO GET THE DETAILS OF A PROSPECT IN THE FACE OF AN IMPENETRABLE GATEKEEPER

Sometimes you can hit a brick wall in your attempts to phone a prospect. You may encounter an impenetrable gatekeeper, and all your online searches turn up empty. These tips can help you scale that wall.

Call other extensions in the same office and discover a way to get to know the name and title of your prospect with whoever lands on the other end of the call.

Get help from their sales team. Just be honest direct and polite.

Go around back if you've visited the office in person. Try to reach out to other people likely to be on break or handling other matters in the vicinity. Remember to be polite, non-aggressive and honest.

Finally, be persistent. As the saying goes, persistence wears resistance, your persistence is what counts.

WHY SALESPEOPLE MAKE IPP A PRIMARY PROSPECTING APPROACH

There are some salespeople who, in this age of unprecedented connectivity, focus on in-person prospecting as a primary approach to prospecting. They deceive themselves by believing that pointless roaming or driving around their territories somehow works. Also, some salespeople stick to this approach because they have sales managers who say that good salespeople are the ones whom they cannot see in the office. However, most do it because they are just afraid or unable to use the phone and bury their heads in the excuse of "I'm just better in person."

"Consistently relying on a single prospecting methodology (usually the one you feel generates the least amount of resistance and rejection), at the expense of others, consistently generates mediocre results" (Blount, p. 21).

PLANNING FOR E-MAIL PROSPECTING

Planning for email prospecting is a rule, not an exception. Failure to plan results in bad emails which destroy your credibility and tarnish your brand. It is paramount to prepare before you embark on email prospecting.

When planning, first you must consider your audience. Consider whom you are writing to and ask yourself questions that will help you draft an appropriate message. Then you must determine your method, which must be suited for your audience and can deliver your purpose. Thirdly, customize your message to your audience. Do this by stepping in their shoes, getting their perspective of what is essential, and what will drive them to take action. Lastly, define your goal. You cannot hit or ask for an unknown objective.

HOW TO STRUCTURE EFFECTIVE TEXT MESSAGES

Text message prospecting is a potent tool to add to your arsenal. However, it is an invasion of the prospect's personal space; therefore, familiarity is critical. Whenever you are up for text prospecting, these rules will keep you from derailing into getting blocked by your prospect.

1. Identify yourself. It is likely that the prospect didn't save your number after the event where you met or after the introduction. Therefore they may need a short, polite reminder.

2. Craft a message that the reader can easily understand and is relevant to them.

3. Be succinct.

4. Avoid using abbreviations and emoticons, your message should be professional.

5. Use a transparent link where links are necessary.

6. Re-read before you send.

7. Keep track of your text messages. Remember, sales are scientific.

FOUR PILLARS OF MENTAL TOUGHNESS IN SALES

Mental toughness is a critical ingredient for fanatical prospectors. Anyone can learn it by basing his or her steps on the following foundations.

Desire: Not a hope or a wish but an active aspiration that rises above everything. To know how strong your desire is, ask yourself what do you want? How do you plan to get it? How badly do you want it?

Mental Resilience: A constant investment in yourself and your mental capacities. As you grow in resilience, you apply less effort and get better results.

Outlearning: Gaining more knowledge through reading and devouring other resources enables salespeople to see the world differently, become more resourceful, have better conversations with their prospects, and eventually out-earn their competitors.

Physical resilience: Physical resilience regulates mental vitality. When you are in excellent physical condition, you think better, with more clarity, and become more optimistic. You have to eat well, get enough sleep, and exercise.

EDITORIAL REVIEW

Fanatical Prospecting promises solutions to unlock sales conversations and fill sales pipelines. Jeb Blount, a veteran salesperson, anticipates early skepticism on the subject matter and lays out a review which opines that the advice contained in the book is not idealistic or academic but a practical step-by-step guide for practicing salespeople. His place as one of the top sales leaders of the decade lays credence to this assertion.

Like an expert coach, the reader goes through the first half of the book with short chapters organized as quick wins. A staunch believer in the concept of "no pain no gain" Blount describes different types of salespeople and poses a question to the reader: what makes superstar salespeople extraordinary? Authoritatively focusing on the central problem of organizations in the midst of sales challenges, he assertively shoots down emerging arguments purporting that cold calling and telephone prospecting are outdated. He expertly highlights what threatens a sales pipeline using his experiences to show how each threat can take root and crystallize.

A veteran salesperson, sales leader and successful entrepreneur, Blount gives insightful tips on prospecting from the different perspectives of a salesperson, the sales manager and the prospect. He demonstrates that his advice works and skillfully enriches the content with captions and quotes from other writers including respectable business publications such as the *Harvard Business Review*. He also cites various scientific studies. Blount includes several anecdotes from past experiences in business and other social settings to engage the reader and provide further support for his arguments.

Some of the anecdotes, however, are quite lengthy, which could distract the reader from the main point. At times, one can't help but wonder if the book is a marketing tactic for LinkedIn as Blount endlessly praises the social platform. Blount then diverts from the sales process and elements of winning sales strategies towards coaching the salesperson into the characteristics they should adopt. He clearly describes the attributes of winning salespeople, and the specific actions you can take to experience transformation. He shares his turning point, which motivates the reader into excelling.

Fanatical Prospecting is a brief but powerful wake-up call to any salesperson or team leader. It provides insight at all levels, and the author does well to provide links for further exploration, tools, and resources. At the end of it all, *Fanatical Prospecting* is an accurate guide to having authentic sales conversation and excelling in sales, no matter what industry you may be in.

BACKGROUND ON AUTHOR

Jeb Blount is an accomplished salesperson, sales leader and entrepreneur. He has been in sales for over 25 years and runs three companies, Sales Gravy, Channel EQ and Innovate Knowledge. He is also an accomplished speaker having trained several fortune 500 companies and a respected author with seven titles under his belt and a large following, exceeding 225,000 people, of his weekly newsletter. He has received several accolades for his endeavors and has been distinguished in various publications including *Top Sales Magazine*, *Forbes* and *The Huffington Post*. He and his wife Carrie have a teenage son, and they live in South Georgia.

Other Titles by Jeb Blount

People Love You: The Real Secret to Delivering a Legendary Customer Experience (John Wiley & Sons, 2013)

People Follow You: The Real Secret to What Matters Most in Leadership (John Wiley & Sons, 2011)

People Buy You: The Real Secret to What Matters Most in Business (John Wiley & Sons, 2010)

Sales Guy's 7 Rules for Outselling the Recession (Macmillan 2009)

Business Expert Guide to Small Business Success (Business Expert Publishing, 2009)

Power Principles (Palm Tree Press, 2007).

*** END OF BOOK SUMMARY***

*If you enjoyed this **ZIP Reads** publication, we encourage you to purchase a copy of the original book.*

We'd also love an honest review on Amazon.com!

*ZIP*READS

Made in the USA
Monee, IL
08 February 2024